SIGHT LINES

Also by Charlotte Mandel

The Marriages of Jacob
Keeping Him Alive
The Life of Mary
Doll
A Disc of Clear Water
Saturday's Women
(editor, with Maxine Silverman and Rachel Hadas)

SIGHT LINES

poems by

Charlotte Mandel

photographs by

Judy Seigel

MIDMARCH ARTS PRESS
New York City

Library of Congress Catalog Card Number 97-075904
ISBN 1-877675-27-X

Printed in the United States of America

Midmarch Arts Press
300 Riverside Drive
New York, New York 10025

For Manny
our children
and grandchildren

Acknowledgements

I am grateful to the editors of magazines in which the following poems first appeared, sometimes in slightly different form: *Seneca Review*: "Table for Four"; *River Styx*: "Collecting Tinfoil"; *Nimrod International Journal of Prose and Poetry*: "To Pass the Time"; *West Branch*: "A Cousin Comes to Me," "Touring the Mill," "Coordinates"; *Puckerbrush Review*: "Yard Song"; *Stone Country*: "Bahia"; *Paterson Literary Review*: "The Children's Science Museum," "Painting the Sea," "Baby Boomlet on My Block"; *In the West of Ireland*: "The World Is a Greenhouse"; *Spirit That Moves Us*: "Rosie to Her Daughter"; *Lips*: "Birthday in Three-Quarter Time"; *The Gopherwood Review:* "Mammography"; *US 1 Worksheets*: "Child at Flood Tide"; *Jewish Women's Literary Annual*: "Sonogram," "Daily Visitor." "Approaching Blindness" first appeared in *New Millenium Writings*, Winter 1997, Vol. 2, Issue 2. "Honing" returns from my first collection, *A Disc of Clear Water*. "Table for Four" is reprinted in *Anthology of Magazine Verse & Yearbook of American Poetry*.

"Last Bend in the Tunnel of Love" was awarded the Norma Farber Award by the New England Poetry Club.

"Painting the Sea" has been set to music by Robert Convery, first performed by Paul Sperry at Museum of the City of New York.

For their gifts of uninterrupted time and place for work at various seasons in recent and past years, I am grateful to the Corporation of Yaddo, the Virginia Colony for Creative Arts, Villa Montalvo Center for the Arts, The Millay Colony, and the hospitality of the Rockefeller Foundation at Bellagio. Thanks also to the Geraldine E. Dodge Foundation which sponsored one of my residencies at Yaddo.

Special thanks to Colette Inez, and to Anneliese Wagner, for generous encouragement and critical comment on poems in progress; and to my editor, Cynthia Navaretta, for clearsighted guidance.

CONTENTS

I

HONING

The kitchen's electric clock mimes the rasp of
breadknife honed on an oval stone rod.
This was my mother's stone,
black rubbing to gray, worn
like cheekbones on an elongated blind
face through all the working
years of her life.

Women are always working their hands —
the knitting lacing hands probing
like freshets of water for energy, motion
sounding the birth of faces. Women have always
flowed upon stone,

persistences of their bodies like knives
made of water carving as they
are sharpened, oblique blades
cutting the twelve striations of wheel
into channels

that rock may breathe
sun coming alive
chips of light
skipping water
surface to surface
skinning the earth

COLLECTING TINFOIL

Combing the alley, I hunched
my shoulders and crimped my mouth,
took small steps too slow
for streetside dealings
in baseball cards and cellophane bags
of marbles. Winners riffled
stacks of phototickets or knuckled
glass immies fast as bullets

but I was a collector of tinfoil, one
in a straggle of loners, hunter-gatherers
picking empty packs of cigarettes and gum.
Our goal to peel the metal liner intact,
spread the leaf
easy as a tongue over a globe of ice cream
upon the enlarging nugget, a labor
of weeks and months
for the diameter
of an eye.

Utmost size was infinity — a word
I'd been taught to mean
there was no end ever
to more. The ball existed, matter
glistening
of nothing but itself, an integrity.

Inside ourselves were uncontrollable
organs lined with waving cilia,
shapes like swollen squids were
crushing our food, permeating
our skins with indelible scent.
The war came sniffing.

Somewhere within the long guns,
my crinkled tin leaf
could spring a thousand triggers,
flare red rocket barrage in the dawn's
early light. Swift
uniformed children set to the gleaning
of wrappers fallen in the streets.

Before my uncles sailed or flew across oceans,
they patted me on the shoulder,
saved for me
empty packs fragrant
with bits of tobacco.
It was for their sake, they said,
I hunted camels luckies old golds.
The ball given form by the fingers
and palms of my hands
batted itself off to ring the war's end
as the whistling world

shattered indivisibles.
Brand new particles
sifted through the sieves
of our skins,
buffing the old parts of bodies aglow,
live metallic air
collecting the luster at will.

NATIONAL DAY OF MOURNING

for Oklahoma City, April 19, 1995

Soot swirls across the cities. At half mast,
limp stripes stroke the poles, stars blink smoke-dried tears
for Baylie, her doll-limbs of bloodied silk
spilling drops like a breast too full of milk.
Mouth on the insuck of a scream, her bier
grimed rescuer's arm, her dirge deafening blast.

Spring. The maple like a cheer leader shakes
clusters of yellow papery fringe, fresh
beginnings of pods — light propeller wings
children pinch onto noses, march and sing,
chins tilted. Squirrels go drunk on green flesh,
juice-filled kernels. Lawns quiver under rakes.

Street chase: tricycles firing pistol caps.
On screen: Roll call Flowers Teddy bears Taps.

YARD SONG

Barberry hedge flutters, mocking
bird mimics finch, purple
rhododendron shakes a rattle
of bird calls, overhead
serrate blade in the throat
of a bluejay, the constant
beckon of robins   *I'm here*
I'm here

On the holding pedal of memory, trills
course through the wires
of a sparkling cage —
my mother's fist
once a week scoured
the swinging perches
smeary gravel ground
hot yellow feathers forced meanwhile
to a cramped wooden pillory
canary screaming in chirps
though my lips were near *birdie*
birdie I'm here

and yet would sing released
in its nave of sky
wild cannabis fed.

From the white pines that shield
my yard from the red brick
nursing home where in a hoarse
and breathless summer I used
my teeth to snip

blossoms for the vase with painted
flying crane on the sill
of my mother's room

the monotone
alms-begging *give? give?*
of a mourning dove.

TIME CHANGE: DAYLIGHT SAVING: FIFTH AVENUE

Noon glare at 5 o'clock rush hour
jump-starts a dance of shoulders.
I dodge like a boxer, attach
to a zigzag line for pizza —
my appetite's out of joint,
circadian gravity in free fall.

The sky keeps time in a rolling
steeplechase of clouds.
Do we ride the curve of some primordial throw —
the ball studded with four billion of us,
feet on the ground, heads in the air
in all directions swearing
we know the way up and face
forward on the carousel,
one-way breeze scoring years into skin?

I'm out of breath in a universe
of shop windows, running in place
opposite a form swaddled in army blankets,
bare arm extending a styrofoam cup,

who stands like a zodiac sign
that's suddenly mine.

Digits blink red in the sunset —
hour: minute: second.
Shards of the last rays
singe the mannequins' eyes
open twenty-four hours a day.

24 HOUR MONITOR

A pillow between us
muffles battery-driven
ink stabs and wavering retreats —
rhythm of your heart's double-speak.
My fingers hover, illiterate
above taped conductor discs.
The monitor's scroll unwinds,
rewinds.

In my dream, you turn
like the wooden spoke inside a torah
beginning yearly repetition
of the Books. Towards you the beautiful
letters open and disappear
clothing you in blank parchment.

A sacred scroll unwinds to be sung.
You murmur
a catalog of chemical equations.
A bell without a tongue
calls the hours,
bone marrow exchanges
cell by cell
plasma for stone.

Asleep, we fall
through the sieve of language.
Our arms across the ticking box
embrace
the trapped verb of your heart.

NOTES FROM THE CARDIAC WING,
DALLAS

        "Snow,"
I write — antonym of Dallas,
city of heat, city where the battery of a president's death
recharges — Dallas where I have shot
by airplane
              your bed the axis of a white room
sky advertising puffs of cloud
white as first of the season
New York City snow flakes
        magic for complexions
        mother would scrub my face with bees of ice,
        seizing swarms
        through the fire escape window

Impossible to placate
a handful of snow, it numbs
slips through fingers

I go on
sitting here, watching you
sleep, yearning to climb under your cover,
lie with you, numb,
enclose the lifetime body of our love
within this hospital's hum
of drawling courteous voices.
Yet I nurse the fact of my shivering,
bind knots of pain like a life rope
against slide into freezing
sleep.

       *

Night. I pass through the corridor
of newborns. Beyond the glass wall,
a girl with slim fingers winding
strands of air,
tiny triangular mouth
memorizing a bubble of water —
born to introspect

Another whose fat frog legs still punch
exit through a fleshy sack,
black-fringed blue gaze
daring me to make a move

Citizens slid into Dallas
barely an hour,
moisture of first breaths
glistening
upon the sound-porous glass

Their mewings echo sighs
of my chest rising falling

       sleet
       again
       my face aglow with snow melt

WAITING FOR ORDERS

Hoping to break the code, we watch
the half-open starry blinks of her eyelids.
Oldest in evolution, the reptile brain
dies last. Chains of taut
synaptic wire snap.
Heart and lungs transact in peace
the business of letting go.

Nurses come with brisk
and humble hands
seeking her veins. She who has been
their scientific oracle —
touchstone to healing —

races her eyes back and forth as if
reading space between our bodies.
Does she
memorize a diagram —
blueprints projected on a screen —
arrows pointing to
"Cause" "Reason"?

    Dearest
helpmates — like porters, you want to carry
this case packed with my rage
and your fears.
Don't pray — I go from, not to.
Not on wings —
this bed transports me.
Stroke the cramp in my legs.
Speak to each other.

COORDINATES

The sun
burning out of control
a hell in blue heaven
beyond the wakes
of grasshopper jets

Obedient moon
drawn to our magnet
beautiful
through no intention of its own

Earth
hour by hour twirling clouds
no more than mist
we comb through our fingers
Patches of forest, rock, glacier
stitched to a core of lava

This morning
the shock of E's name in print
on the obituary page. Tomorrow

our circle of friends
clasping two-handed as though
caught in midair

scanning the tunnels of each other's eyes
for a glimpse of her

only to see mirrored
the space
which has room for us.

THE CHILDREN'S SCIENCE MUSEUM

Pummeled by street winds, children
revolve through the doors, land
in the cloakroom and shed pillow jackets

into coded vinyl baskets, one per family.
Live water runs down the artificial mill.
Shouting, they dabble, splashing

instructive signs the parents read aloud.
In the theater of HOW WE HEAR,
pushbuttons trigger their squeals

along with moose calls, barks and bleats.
But in the bleached HALL OF SKELETONS,
glass boxes sound-proof

the pronged coiling spine of COBRA,
quilled hump of HEDGEHOG.
Look up: from the ceiling's high dome

hangs Halloween's familiar, a skeleton
labelled: MAN. Look down:
a bell jar at child's eye level

compares erect HUMAN INFANT.
A bolt secures the fontanel to a steel rod
fitted through skull, rib cage,

and butterfly pelvis, to stand
limbs on tips of ten white thorns.
Stroller wheels screech

into reverse — babies
slung into denim knapsacks, heels thumping
the muscular backs of fathers,

wave as white sculptures dance away.
Siblings race to the human heart
big as a room.

Tunneling through red-lit amplified pulse-rock,
hands on their chests,
"Boom," they sing, "Boom!"

II

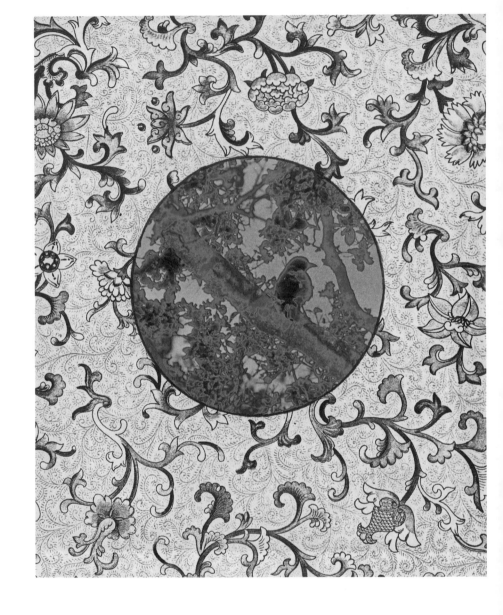

AN ALEPH-BEIT OF TRINKETS

To Martin Tucker,
for a gift of his late mother's costume jewelry

   i Bracelet

Does this dangle-disc of gold
filigree encircling
flowing Hebrew letters,
read:
     SHALOM or *MAZEL?*

Which blessing do I fetter by a chain
to my wrist?

In ages past, our scribes' long beards
swept the parchment
scattering dots and dashes of vowels
away like gnats annoying the feet
of stately consonants —

a habit that has gifted us with
poster decor, trinkets, charms
and apples of discord/enlightenment —
pilpul based on optical illusions —

this way that way
like steps of the hora in a ring
stamping for every bride and groom
the music of peace and good fortune
good fortune and peace.

ii Brooch

Upright lions of Judah —
heraldic bookends —
with front paws and a hind foot
supporting a torah scroll,
tongues uncurling to taste
the sweetness of Hebrew alphabet.

"aleph beis gimel dallet" recited
Reb Appleman, my tutor who stood
no taller than I at eleven.
Roundbellied apple-man, white beard
and pink cheeks, trying to implant
seed from his tree of knowledge.

Line by line in Yiddish,
we studied *Genesis*,
I reading aloud:
"*adom hot derkent zein veib chaveh*"
he translating
with an instant's pause that alerted
my nose to the scent of adults dissembling:
"Adam, he, uh, *know* his wife, Chaveh."

I, with the patronizing shrug
of an American-born
toward textual redundancy (of course
the couple already "knew" each other),
continued: "*und zie is trogendik gevoren.*"
Reb Appleman humhummed, turned the page, and I
respectfully silent,
knew
Adam's wife had conceived.

iii Pendant

Onto the desk, toss
the jingling weight

Heads up!
study the portico of a temple gate
from which a handkerchief leads the dance —

CHAI

LIFE

fired on an anvil
no bigger than a petri dish

written in sparks
swirls of constellary smoke

thirteen moons
shiny as brass — I caught
the one called *Nisan*
spinning towards my Shabbot
birth — and screamed
not with fear but to expel
thunderclap chill
inhale / exhale

while the shocked soul
climbed the V of my breastbone,
panting.

A COUSIN COMES TO ME

As though the Red Sea roars on Times Square
we race to the shore
of each other's arms. "*Vie shain du bist,*"

I say, my tongue amazed by dormant
nursery Yiddish. You are my age, Rochel,
daughter of Nuchim, who was brother of

Rochel, my mother. In Israel, you've raised
two daughters and a son,
as I have done. I am afraid of you.

Leading you to Port Authority,
I inventory traits: the curly hair
and sparrow gait of Tante Clara,

eyebrow shrug of great-aunt Reiter.
They died as my mother — at last,
in nursing homes, confused by care. You lived:

in the camps, you sorted coats, blouses, boots,
felt hats. You are my last
first cousin. On the bus, I pry a young girl's

outline from your form — the photograph on grainy
dark stock — foreign, square-breasted, poor.
We locked our door. You have not shared my family

of misers, hoarders of betrayals, slammers
of windows cracked by knuckles of reproach.
Wary, I lean to your ironic lilt,

the tone that filled my childhood rooms. Visitor
from a desert, you gasp at the June green
of my lawn. Soon you will see my appliances

pumping out water, half-breads
forgotten in the box, jars, foils spread
as though paper and plastic were air.

Translating your silence, I hear, "You did
nothing to deserve better luck than I —
you were safe — you let us die."

I turn my key in the door. Sun points to the dust
aroused. On a long, deep breath, you say,
"Oh my cousin, how beautiful is your house."

ROSIE TO HER DAUGHTER

An old Russian woman and I
were the only ones not seasick.
God rolled that boat on the ocean
like a dreidl. Grandfather kissed me

goodbye with the tips of his fingers —
from his lips to my forehead up
to the mezuzah on the door.
For him, I, too, was holy.

But only men could read prayers.
It was in Yiddish that your
Tante Clara wrote, "Come
to me and Paul in America."
We slept in back of the store.

A sister isn't a mother.
A girl like a horse, she wanted.
My back and my arms remember
the butter we dug from barrels,
the flour and onions in sacks.

Better to board with strangers.
In the pencil factory, all
the Gentile girls loved my blond hair!
"Rosie, you are not really Jewish."

How that Sally could write letters!
"Come on, put some real stuff in it."
To your father, she mixed in words
that kissed from the pages — and signed

"Rose." Do you know when he first saw
my writing? On the marriage license!

I gave you an American father
and Yiddish lessons after school
so you can read a letter from me
if you go away. I showed you off

at four — you wrote your whole name
with chalk on the sidewalk. But you
study so hard. Don't hurt your eyes.
No one will care about you
the same as a mother.

CHILD AT FLOOD TIDE

My heels dug in
toes clamped like snails
to the scurrying sand bed.
Knotted ropes of water
dragged off sand
shaping a pyramid I balanced on.
The longer I stood
the higher my pedestal rose
yet the deeper I sank

as though the tide itself
pounded the nail of my body
to a root-stem of earth
that could not be swallowed away
as long I stood in place
a living jetty against breakers
pulling castles shells and children
back to the oncoming swell

I was holding, holding
shrill throat crying down the roar
of wave after wave
foaming at my thighs
belly, waist —

until a hammer-
claw grip plucked me
into the air, high spray
salt as spittle in my face

and the man who thought he saved me
did not know I wept
against the thudding
heart in his chest

for the churning ground
I would never get back.

BAHIA

Crayon the equator red: fever is normal.
A dugout canoe slices the mango sun.

Gold leaf immerses the altar and nave,
all but her face and his body of enamel.

I would give the begging child money if his scabs
didn't look like the sores on the street dog's flanks.

A trawler of singers strums the moon's orange wake.
Hands flutter like pennants from the hotel balconies.

My necklace of flowers smells brackish.
The iron grille presses orchids on my forehead.

FOR MEI LING, FLOWERS OF WHITE RIBBON

Back from Disneyworld — "You haven't gone?
Go!" Round as a child's drawing of the sun,
my neighbor's amber cheeks cuddled dimples
under glossy black bangs cut in simple
schoolgirl style. In pink hard hat, her daughter
one-stepped between our lawns on a scooter
just bought. Her son, blase, popped a wheelie —
bicycle and headgear glittering steely
Star-trek black —

      "The wages of sin is death,"
intones the Reverend's sing-song Chinese —
a woman translates, phrase by phrase.
Pungent chrysanthemum, lily, baby's breath,
and food — ghosts have gnawing stomachs. Banquette
cloth, roast chicken, fruit. White mourning rosette
pinned to the little girl's hair. Child's weeping
stubborn antiphony to sung hymn. . . . *Why?*
In the sweet by and by. . . .
           "Sin is why we die."
Fairy tale reversed — Beauty lies sleeping
after the happy ending. What tonic kiss
mends an artery burst? Sound tapes hiss
to the serpent's magnified maddened
y-tipped cartoon tongue in Disney's *Aladdin.*

BABY BOOMLET ON MY BLOCK

Bicycles darting like fish,
the racers with ladybug
shells on their heads
splash into automatic sprays —
parched lawns divided by asphalt
shiny and black as a river —
the world of my street
where showers of memory revive

my ginger-boy in a pompom hat
pedalling his fraction of empire
in a chevy-blue car, rubber horn
honking howdy-doody soundtrack —
get-out-of-my-way!

Ginger man with a bearded smile,
going seventy on the freeway —
Hi Mom by cellular phone
What's the coast to coast news?

      It cost us a hundred dollars
to have the cedar cut down
planted the year you were born.
Branches clawed the car's fenders
going in and out the garage. Roots
pried up and cracked the corner
foundation. Arctic storms
last winter — the snowplow and salt
gouged a crevasse into our driveway.
I swear we'll need
crampons and a rope halter
if it happens again.

I don't tell him each time I back down
that angle to the street,
I'm terrified
I might kill a child —
so many so fast, they disappear into
the blind side — I hang there
caught with the brake engaged.

NEWSPRINT

Warm skin activates the ink —
your innocent hands pass soot
like Midas his gold.
Take this

fingerprint left on the cheek
of the newsphoto child
whose spindly neck
sticks up

from the khaki shirt grazing
her ankles, knobby
as joints of bamboo,
whose toes

splay in over-sized flip-flops,
the ones her mother's feet
kicked upside down when
soldiers

sprayed bullets like gardeners watering
a golf course.
                    Sundays, you turn
glossy

magazine pages. Ipanema's ripples,
lobsters, curries and vodkas
flash disco lights into
your eyes

reflecting ecstacies to sweat for.
Yet the little girl's cheek
identifies the print
cross-filed

with your passport signature
and photograph
superimposed upon
her face.

BOY FALLS TO DEATH
IN NEW JERSEY SINKHOLE

(headline, *The New York Times*)

"I'm hungry!" seven nights he had screamed
in his sleep — eyelids squeezed shut,
cheeks sucked against baby molars.
Thrashing feet woke his older brother
mummy-trapped in their quilt.
For seven nights, his dreambody
stared at the gaping bowl of his stomach
craving to be filled although in the morning
his mother's skillet sang
and he doodled syrup tentacles on toast,
drank milk if she urged.

And when their backyard sank,
his tall brother who scored drop shots
fast as the electronic board could switch numbers
bellywhopped and got him by the wrist
while another kid ran for help and the father
came, but by then the palms of both boys' hands
were fastened on dirt. The younger son's
cowboy belt buckle incised a whinnying track
downward downward

*

Rim of starry blackness arches above far cliffs,
rivers and pools reflect chalk-grey
overhanging branches, voices

of his brother, father, mother
wrap him in a scarf of cobwebs.
Children examine him through eyes
of forgotten colors.
Memories jostle like popping beads.

When fruit appears he eats core, seeds, skin.
One day, another child
comes sliding
scrabbling for roots.
The boy strokes the newcomer's hair.
Yes, they form pairs.
He is no longer the odd one, last chosen
to speak for the earth.

BIRD-BOY: EVE REMEMBERING ABEL

I could have killed him
that time —
"Ma-a, watch me fly!"
His knuckly toes
gripped the edge of the quarry
Vertical drop
to the gloating green eye of water
I saw his shirt fly off
his navel, the dimple and crack
of flat buttocks

Every mother carries murder in her heart
"Ma-a, look at me-e . . ."
arms outstretched like the flight bones
of a bat's skeleton

I was screaming his name by then
breath spurting from my mouth like blood
I stood too far below to stop him in time
too far above the water to race down
billow the safety net of my skirt
"Ma-a, look at me-e . . ."

His name
wailing thin from my lungs

Into the air he leapt
arc of an eagle
his cry a mosquito whine

"A-a-a-be-l-l . . ."
mocked back from the stones
like bursts of laughter.

Bird-boy
silhouetted
on water
divided the gleaming surface
and came
gliding the way a web-footed bird
seems to propel with its belly.

I wanted to beat him for my gasping heart.
Perched to dry in the sun, he cocked his head —
"Tell me a story about
when you were a little girl."

There is no such story.
No childhood begins me.
I thought story was mine to create
by what I lived.

Abel my son
knew himself invulnerable
to powers of rock, water, a mother's
righteous blows, her rebel's
rage against the story-weaver
who had named him
the one who would be killed by his brother.

THE WORLD IS A GREENHOUSE

The arctic shrugs
sloughs off
glaciers easily as paper
pillars in a Hollywood biblical epic.

Ultraviolet blisters
the cosmic membrane
still pale blue
as the eyes of newborns
reflecting a planet
wrapped in its rightful caul.

We are immigrants
transported
to a galaxy
that mimics the familiar
row of split-level houses

but the doors
have no thresholds,
roofs hum
air is pulled into orbit
and walls ring like glass
as once an oriole flew
into greenery's double
that shimmered in the picture window.

Listen to the chimes of breaking.
Sing to the child in your arms:
Bless this house that rocks me
like an iron lung.

III

BIRTHDAY IN THREE-QUARTER TIME

Sailing on applause, his wheelchair
draws a multicolored wake of balloons.
Skeletal and smiling, Louis lifts his chin
like an actor about to recite.
A member of the nursery class
who visit aged folks on Wednesday
offers a bouquet of cut and pasted tulips.
He kisses dimples on the back of her hand,
waves in the air
an engraved 100th birthday card
from Mr. and Mrs. President of the United States.

The paralyzed reach clawed hands
towards the daughter with a silver knife
slicing the whipped cream roses
and swirled capital "L" of his name.
Lipless mouths open to plastic forks
opulent with chocolate.
The woman in bulgy cotton socks
who's never uttered a word
embraces the oak spinet and asks,
"What shall I play?"
   Happy Birthday
leaps hop scotch along chipped keys,
doughy fingers segue into *Harvest Moon Bye Bye Blackbird*
and quit.
Louis totters over, his hands remember
   Blue Danube Let me call you Daisy Daisy
Waltzes guided by his ear revolve the cogs and springs of chairs,
spinning with time as partner,
the humming room his music box.

LAST BEND IN THE TUNNEL OF LOVE

Oh my friend — your voice speaks out of a crazy-
house waxwork skeleton. I offer daisies
trembling on their stems. The cuckoo clock
springs a fanged bat — flying vampire that mocks
your torpid remnant of blood. "Forgive
my closed eyes — go on — talk is curative —
conjure me a gorgeous car." Only skin
retains you, long bone, and listening brain.
Electric candles blink in a nailed sconce.
Talk flickers, dear psychoanalyst. Nonce
forms dictate sentences "until you get
your strength back." Your wife pats the coverlet,
rubbing, rubbing, her palms reading engraved
words set to the pulse of loved body saved.

PAINTING THE SEA

My daughter painted a seascape the day
she was twelve. She shows a gifted hand.
(Can you find the right door — where is the way

we came in?) Corkscrew shadow marks the quay,
cross-hatching the nets. Her brush quiet as sand,
my daughter painted the sea on a day

the sun wove yellow through a bluegreen bay,
her sailboat still as a lullaby's end.
(Can you find the right door — where is the way

we came in?) How could she guess the interplay
of moon with undertow, caprice of wind?
My daughter flew this pennant on a day

clouds blossomed to roses — your white bouquet
resembles that shape in her sky. She signed —
can you find her name? the year? — in the way

an artist initials the future. Pray
if you know the rules. Will you walk behind
my daughter? She painted the sea that day
on a wind's trap door. Please — come — here's the way.

TABLE FOR FOUR

Sharpen a sepia pencil to define
her slim economy of cheek, tennis-
trained quick turn of chin, green feline
irises, curious and free of menace.

For him, a blunt stub of charcoal to catch
in choppy moves of thumb against index,
the bristle of tweed and grizzled rough thatch
of beard, not unbarbered — his style a mix

of proletarian/academic thirsts.
In their fifties, planning to marry,
both widowed, fallen into love at first —
just that — sight. In the confectionary

of their constant handholding, Bill and I,
who loved him and his wife for twenty years,
drink too much wine. We long to fortify
their happiness, but simply disappear

as ravelings tucked in their frame of bliss,
specks in the background wash of her/friends/his.

DAILY VISITOR

Isidore, a hundred and one,
totters past like a limping sparrow.
Women doze in Queen Anne chairs, half-molted
feathers of white caressing pink scalps.
My father, ninety-eight, will be
upstairs, re-reading I. B. Singer.
His nostrils no longer translate
kitchen aroma of simmering chocolate

to memories of schoolchildren,
my mother's hand or mine
stirring dark sweet lava.
Each day as I breathe at the entrance,
oven or burner wafts another reading
of my life, seasons of preparation.

      That's Louie's daughter
somebody says, the words
rumoring through walls.
As though the house itself
knows my step, boards creak
with expectant nods.
Up the stairs, whispers
precede me like applause.

On the day of my final visit
I shall climb to where my father
sits in his room
          and across the hall,
a vacant room will be ready —

my clean underwear in the drawer,
print dresses in the closet,
a too-large pink comb resting
on a tatted dresser scarf. A bed,
a chair.

I'm Louie's daughter
I murmur to the bent-over woman
in the maple-framed mirror.
My father's face has never wrinkled.
Sit down,
he says, *sit down.*

ARRANGING THE STILL LIFE

Each facet of cut glass vase
seizes image:
             pheasant's eye, half-open,
             tinge of amber sunlight
             through a square window
Mites of dried blood sift
onto the copper tray's bluegreen patina,
spatter brown and vermilion.
The bird's umber stare
refuses reflection of the man's face —
without gloss, there is no play.
The artist knows how water teases
form through skirrings of leaves
and sway of green inchworm silk,
how odd gusts of air
ratify shadows — light is a trickster
he ties to his brush.

He chooses the bluegreen robin's egg
cracked by a cuckoo's beak.
From the ochre gel within,
stench rises. A sudden
sprig of lilac
branches out of the vase
another and another

skewer of his brush pinning
showers of roseblue
to the canvas, each petal
tense within white, his fingers
so quick they blur.

JESSICA'S CHAIR

A large club,
upholstered in orange/fuschia
Bauhaus print, dimmed with years
of her muscles slackening, disarrayed
with tremor.
No one has plumped up the cushions.

Threads of cording on the left arm
mark the clip-on tray
for books no longer held, plastic
drinking straws bent
towards her lips.
A darkened patch records
the height of her head,
the skirt's tear
gauges the bumper
of the motorized wheelchair
dismantled in the next room.

On four walls around us, her paintings
swirl into galaxies
frame by frame — intensities of color
she'd found by paring earth's crust
with her fingers —

      (I was a beginner at reading art —
      I don't see my world, Jessica.
      Her arms lifted like a candelabrum —
      Come into my world!)

The chair is the largest in the room
and everyone sits somewhere else
until one of the cousins,

a trim, travelled journalist
curls into the worn fabric,
crosses her legs with the ease
of her television fame

talks of her voyage across
the Equator, the sight of the ship's flag
and her own hands in the air
outlined in St. Elmo's fire —

And after she leaves, Jessica's husband
sinks into the chair,
takes tobacco from a wrinkled leather pouch,
strikes a match,
and lights his pipe.

The paintings smolder, bloom,
oscillate in changes of light,
each of us a sun
as we go on talking.

VISITING LUCIENNE

Shoes set primly on the green
grass carpet, we occupy
a curved row of wicker chairs
like dolls at a tea party, mouths
turned up at the corners,

faced to the billowy chintz
recliner where Lucienne,
her African glow
drained by chemical infusions
to a mummy's parchment,

turns her mouth up at the corners
towards the young mother striding
through the patio doors.
Six month old Lisa, swung
on tennis-muscled arms
down to the carpet, giggles.
Her mother sinks cross-legged and zips
open a quilted yellow satchel.

Spoonful by spoonful,
mashed banana
smacks between plump bubbly lips.
The meaty fragrance of tropical fruit
germinates in the air.

In unison we sway
forward to breathe
what the baby exhales.

SONOGRAM

To a grandchild photographed in utero

We see you, builder
        without hands sorting
                nerve tooth spleen

Without tongue sucking
        milk and honey
                in the blood

Your chosen atoms tick brisk into
aura
                you weave in the bounce
                        of woman-muscle

How you shine in our dark,
        nub of hunger at work —
                there is no mother,

Only terrain — you are
        what you are to be,
                what you were at that

Tsing! when your inaudible bang
        reunited the echoes
                of that clattering

Scramble for foothold
        we call
                the universe

AUTUMN GINGKO

Fluttering
          swarm
blowaway wings
risen on the ground like foam
undulant yellow
wave leading me beside a pasture
stacked with bales of hay.

Gingko, dweller in prehistory,
closest in longevity
to Eden's untasted tree of life.
Genetic blink that mocks us
for original opportunity lost.

Exquisite fan-shaped leaf
springs from shag-bark
shapeless as a buffalo-crone
worn out with calving.
The fruit is abominable —
pulpy viscous eye-on-a-stem
with an olfactory come-on
repellent to human species.

No way to improve it, the way
white-fleshed apple
glistens in market bins,
hybrids color-coded and squared
to fit into a crate.
The wood is hopeless, not to be timbered

like redwood into uniform planks,
or pine whose byproduct sawdust
sanitizes butchers' floors.

It is the leaf
to which our palms extend,
whose stem we spin
between thumb and forefinger
tracing with awe
an edge of sky that billows
in a bat's wing
mantra ray
the surfboarder's try

Wise design
that does not alter
the one leaf
born with memory of flight
the dip and soar of perfect form.

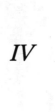

IV

TOURING THE MILL

To a fanfare of crystalled rain,
the canyon unrolls.
Mountains rake the sand from winds into rows
of violet.
The corn is blue.
Women on their knees
build silky blue layers of bread.

On hands and knees we scrape
the round pit of a kiva,
spirit auger to this fourth world.
Sowed by wind, ancient ones
unfolded in caves at eagle height,
the cliffs
borne on shellfish backs.
A history so far in deeds before us
that we stand ashamed, newly
store bought.

Shoppers, we stare at their bones
through plate glass. Colors of jaundice,
mole. A hip labelled rheumatic.
By proxy I shiver

on a sooted limestone shelf, cough
ink smoke.
What could they worship but the ladder world
that lifted
while it ground them to strange evidence?

They were three feet tall,
say descendants who bend to earn
wages at Los Alamos.
One day of the year they dance
soft boots
outdrumming invisible knuckles
within the concrete.
The wind hums still at work
with blue fists paring
the mountain's inner lights.

A cliff of gray mist begins to lock
the deep of the canyon
to the shelf of cloud. Like a fisherman's
vertical net it takes all but the sound
of ocean, diligent
as a woman's arms
driving stone upon corn.

WHITE NOISE

To shake his head only sharpens the fire
alarm embedded within his skull. Mario
used to drum hard rock, ecstatic
mechanical roar
strobe rays hot colors
night gigs, rehearsals, tapes
like pile drivers battering
the ear's helpless auricle
tympanic membrane
nerve piercing brain cortex
until the nerve was honed to scream
days and nights
Mario wears a headset
that plays "white noise"

contrapuntal tuneless croon
spawned in rhythm to microelectonic
couplings muffled by silverquilted walls

Mario's headset sings without lyric,
erases soundtrack he dreams —
crash and surrender of surf, squealing
brakes, women's moans —

Girls in black leather minis shrug with their hips,
dance with each other to get away
from the weirdo guy in his "phones"
get back to the beat, twist and shake
sweat of their turnings amplifies

music gone from Mario's ears
like an artery ripped — pulsating white.

MAMMOGRAPHY

"Take off your shoes,"
says the milk-white technician
fitting a black square plate
into the chromium clip.
I am already naked to the waist

but the table must not be scratched
nor the chained steel door descending
as my body shrinks to a key.
"Lift your elbow, don't move."
Heart and lungs play dead.

Rays indifferent to loveliness
or deformity
ravel a tatter of nipple
infuse the guard of bone.
Begging for love, I offer

my breasts to the god's
hiss of immaculate lightning —
odor of ozone
swirls like incense —
"Don't breathe."

BREEDING STOCK

All around us cows are dropping
calves. This herd went under the stud bull
nine months ago.
Faces white as skulls,
plastic tag stapled to each right ear.
They do not distinguish
me from the men
who jump down from tractors
to count sucklings.
Teeth make a lot of noise
tearing and chomping
clumps of green blades
rampantly manured by bovine
assembly-line stomachs at work.

Their stretched leaking vaginas
have by this time
re-folded. The wobbly black newborns
butt hornless foreheads fiercely
front on to one another and gallop
in circles around their mothers' milk-sacs
re-swelling as fast as calf tongue-and-muzzle
can pump.

I keep a wary distance
as I walk, plugged in to stereophonic
news reporting a milky way of toxins
inhaled and swallowed by soldiers
sent to preserve Kuwait's
bubbling pastures.
The cows bellowing to calves
moan like stepped-on accordions.

At home, a flutist
plays at being a thrush
caroling after storm. The finale
of Beethoven's *Pastorale*
vibrates inside my kitchen radio
beside pale frozen
chunks of supermarket veal
my hand will toss
into seasoned boiling oil.

PLANNING AHEAD

Does this surgical scar predict midwinter
weather of my dying —
clouds dark as battered faces
brooding over stripped trees?

Or will that year like the serpent
biting its tail
circle back, yellow bright
with forsythia,
to April, my birthday?

Wind will scarcely stir for one
pulse erased
from the day's casual
percussions —
                    pause between
adagio andante
blink of red light green

Anticipate by what the body knows —
exact pressures on the skin
of rain dust ice
                    sun blazing

Rope, axe,
crampons for vertical ascent?
Spare canvas, oars,
a brimmed cap for sailing?

What tools should lie to my hand?
What am I to wear?

RE-ENTERING POMPEII

Here, all seasons end save one. I enter
wrapped in the future's invisible mist.
Undulled, time's needle returns to its crack:
Pompeii:
                    a day of perfunctory bows
to seated giants Jupiter and Juno,
sullen on equal thrones. Egyptian Isis
raises rosy breasts aroused by incense.
Chariots stampede an empire's cargo
through the five arched gates, skull-smooth
cobbles whining under iron wheels.
                                    Baths steam
hot swirls of laughter, the jingle of coins,
slithering caress of a slave's oiled palms.
In potters' hands, winejars tall as dancers
whirl to end point. The air's prosperous
stench of tongue-pricking fish sauce
boiling in terra-cotta vats — offal
gutters past — eels' jaws, gills, entrails.
Accustomed nostrils lift, sandals
quickly toe the stepping stones set up
for crossing streets. A breeze sends wolverine
calls of prostitutes, the dock catapults
sailors hard as their oars.
                            Beyond walls,
Vesuvius, wound with trails of donkey carts
spilling grapes about to ferment. Red wine
cools Vulcan's temper — seventeen years
since his iron hammer clawed mosaic floors.

Caverns hold, earth re-seeds. Fire obeys,
licks bowls at altars, cowers in ovens
kindled by fragrant needles of cypress
shading sky-watered slopes of the green hill
humming with bees, gauzed with sperm-rich pollen —
milky wetnurse for whom they slit no throat
of garlanded bull or jeweled heifer —
Vesuvius:

                anchor to life that only a tourist,
zoom lens aimed from the rim of a crater,
bends to, eyes cast down, as to a god.

ONE MORNING

It must be the sickly
light above the mirror of the green
porcelain sink that dissolves
rose tints from her skin
and crimps
her lips into crepe paper folds.
Last week, the doctor found she'd lost
an inch and a half of height.
She leans like a dented umbrella
to brush her teeth, spits
into the drain. Looks up again
at the mouth's angry twist
downward to the side.
She squeezes her eyes tight as a foetus
in the act of being expelled,
head and shoulders bloodied
by tantrum of a womb
cancelling sweet merger,
giving compensation —
breath, light, a self
on loan. Coming due.
Face and body repossessed
against her will, she is bringing
her mother
back from the grave.

TO PASS THE TIME

My mother whose moving lips would trace
captions in the tabloid news

keeps on nodding her head
at my shoulder. Whatever the light —

sun or moon — her shadow
tries the ground ahead of me,

inquisitive as a blind man's cane
tapping, for my sake.

Come — the dark of her head invites,
lays itself down like a cloth —

take a rest from your books,
I have brought you Chinese apples.

But I have been to school and answer,
"No! I won't eat fruit you bring

from a tomb. There has to be a rift
between us. The sun bakes my bread:

I knead words like yeast into the earth —
the letters rise — mouthfuls of light!"

All right — nods the shade — *some people*
play cards —

I stand. My shadow hugs the ground,
picking at stones. The pomegranate cracks

at the press of my thumb. Fluid seeps
thin and red as ink.

Be careful — her voice is kind —
chew on the seeds — *Then spit them out.*

NOTE FROM THE UNRESCUED

Bring fire. Last night's rain
layered a glaze of ice
over the snow.

I have bread. Salt is gone —
futile sprinkle against endless
below zero

skating surface. Bone
slowly ages to lace —
I do not dare

risk falling. Upside down
a squirrel hangs by his nails.
Last sparrow

pecks a bit of dung.
Hickory tree's shell of glass
has not one flaw.

I dreamt a high town
bloomed in water, lily face
at every window.

BAROMETRIC REASONING

Establish fact: a scrim of snow grains
blows at a forty-five degree slant
past the terrace glass doors. Judge
progress of the wind — oddly
silent. Moments ago, shutters'
hinges were screeching
loud as an army of gulls flying
backwards in fear of the sea. Note
use of image: therefore, fiction.
Accustomed birds coast the rhythms
of high swells, enjoy iceberg footholds.
At home. The fear is mine —
of swirls that breath forms,
the letter I'm trying to write to you.
On a line with my pen, a thin pole of oak
bends to sweep the ground,
outermost twigs parted like beaks.
Shall I cry hunger this time, or simply
describe the wind? A long lamenting whine
whips the weathervane. The green
silhouette of a toy whale spins
round, round, and again.

THE BOARD GAME

Her own fault — the game started with her full
consent. Smiling, retying the bow of the blue apron stitched
with red rickrack, she jumped onto the board even before the
first clatter of dice. Arriving so early, she could have taken
dibs on any of the models, but chose this striped bungalow
because it welcomed a single occupant. Now she's trying to
use her body as an eraser to get rid of phrases that seem
stamped onto the walls from reversed print in her brain.
Friction has worn the apron to tatters and her body's friable
and thin. She's gotten the writing down to *Blessed are the* and
Beauty is only and *Better to give than* and *Break, break, thou*

V

SIGHT LINES

for M, on our anniversary

Clamshell   feather   stone   Sea wind
cleansing with sand our faces
alert in a blindfold of mist   White

arch of the world like our wedding
canopy   sight line keeping pace
before us at a footstep's distance

Sea wrack   weed ribbon   moon snail
picked clean   scrap of scuttery crab
discarded   curled feather   stone veined

like a bloodshot eye   Foam
rushes almost to our feet   we swerve
against gravity   The tide at its work

levers   selfwilled
massive crowbar   boulders
pried up loom   ghosts of ships

pounded by breakers   undertow
silent as lungs of a drowned child
Sullen muscular force

of the kindly ocean that taught me to swim
backwards-forwards-cradle
humped unbroken waves   buoyant

nursemaids   godparents
crooning voices I nod to as I hold
cast off shell to my ear   the lobe spackled

with residue of sand that feels to fingertips
like confetti glitter a child will shake
over a surface wetted with glue

Jellyfish squeezes to melt in my fist rubbing
a stone to dry   I walk in step with your form
at low tide looking for signs

Finders keepers bending to pick up
what enters this globe of our seeing
We chart dry land by sound

Boom and fade
Deep held breath and roar
of boundary in love with us

SEA DRIFT

I

It lay on its back
wings spread as in life
climbing wind to the north

Breastbone's marrow still red,
exposed by teeth of scavengers,
cleansed by sand mites.

At the tip of the still feathered neck's
linked chain of bones,
thrown back in denial
or orgasm,
the knob of its skull
thrust a horny fishing beak
into the air

last echo of its "why?"
choked
by sunlight.

II

Soaping last night's
odors of love
from skin and hair, mouth and vulva
bubbling under warm rain, once again

I relish the body's on-the-job attitude
towards keeping me alive — firing sparks
along a tangle of trolley wire nerves
signalling organs to pump,
engulf, expel.

Body, my engineer,
conductor of blood heat,
autonomous believer in the worth
of being's intricate mess —

thanks to you, I wake to read
the digits on my bedside clock
like miraculous letters of light.

III

The cleanliness of death
saves embers
on a winter beach. After burial
in surging turbulence, I would wish to become
sea drift scoured by salt

pristine pebble of bone
rattling to rest
upon the sieve
of a beachcomber seeking coin

or fine grain that whispers
through window screen grid
as through an hourglass.

CALLIGRAPHY LESSON

Look, child, to the bend
of your arm — just so —
the elbow's dimple
shapes the contour
of a closed eye.

Curve your fingers to bridge
the level thumb —
My hand slides a wand
into that half-shell.
Take hold.

For true black,
gaze at a yellow moon
until it melts.
No ink
may flow beyond
the edge of form.

Here is a candle —
open your mouth — the flame
must bow
and return. Use your brush
as breath.

Touch the paper
as flesh.
How fragrant you are.
Follow the stops of my lips
as I speak
into the warm swirl of your ear.

PAINTER'S NOTEBOOK

To Anne Saussois

"Paris is gr-ray!" the consonant growls
from your throat. Across Virginia meadow
you stride into feral explosions of color —
watercolor brush on blue-lined
stenographer pad recording secrets
that summer's toiling green overwashed —
color that crackles, no longer to be sipped.
Root, core and branch done with growing at last.

Your notebook fills reds yellows mauves
Sunlight ignites, sifts through
the two of us. Nimbly over the dawn your plane
will carry this spark of our meeting.
And parting, you tear out a page — fragrance
in a square of paint — breeze
in the tatter of a spiral bound edge —

The forest blazes on my desk consoling
as the trills of wild birds who call
time and place to one another
and do not know that a listener
born singing out of tune
finds harmony *a cappella*
line by page.

AS A CLOUD OF SWIFTS

sang past like a midsummer bell,
papers flew, barometer fell.
Sleeveless I shivered like water
seeping from the icy daughter
spring of the rivulet we'd traced
barefoot on porous limestone laced
with fossil writings, devil-tails
of pre-Cambrian trilobites — failed
species — yet, rhymed in the palms
of our hands — the lines of a psalm —
eddies of moon-drawn motion
salt in us, blue-veined, ocean.

AT THE DOOR OF
THE WRITERS COLONY

Rib to rib, we separate
on a long motionless kiss.
After so many years, our bodies
clasp like hands.
Under this narrow lintel, we brush
against the fact of life as one.

At a stranger's desk, seeking one
perfect metaphor to separate
loss from gain, I cannot brush
away the stunning kiss
of light upon my hand —
the laser pares shell of body

from membrane of mind. Out of body
I travel enclosed, alone.
Time circles and stays. The hands
of my watch touch, then separate
in silence. Your forgotten kiss
flutters on my lips like a brush

I wet with my tongue. Now the brush
tastes of birth — the shock of bodies
split apart. Consoling kiss
upon outraged fontanel — one-
two, one-two — rhythmic separate
fury held in an upturned hand.

The amazing potency of hands —
strokes of the nursery hairbrush
entwining, separating
strands. Adolescent bodies
crave ocean storm at one
turn — at the next, amniotic kiss.

Like cigarette smoke, their kisses
blow past our cheeks. Distant hands
wave cordless telephones.
You and I, tangled underbrush,
tug wiry roots. But here, dream embodies
the page, vibrating, separate.

How shall our bodies kiss
one month from now — lips
brushing lips, hands separate?

SAGAPONACK BEACH

To Hayden Carruth —
"Tell me again how the white heron rises"

My steps the only mark of shoes so far,
the sandbar gives and takes, spongy,
alive. Rows of waterfall glide to shore.

Fencing wire and cries of hatchlings warn
dune grass nesting plover. Farther on, aura
shimmers — a stillwater mirror, newborn

rain pond where six white herons pose like vases
to be dipped and filled with underwater selves.
Thirst dares me too close — a long neck rises —

archangelic wings unfold and flare.
Water scatters image of flight reversed.
My arms carve a zero in feathered air.

AT THE SPEED OF EARTH

Leaves of eucalyptus distill spice
into parched air
and like the blessing of answer
to unspoken question,
rays of California dawn
outline my hands on typewriter keys
recalling chill eastern pasture,
black and white heifers tinted false rose
until the day disc drilled
through granite summit,
light rinsing streaks of afterglow
from the truer fact of blue.

Westward, the continent
hones the sun rising over and over.
At the speed of earth, a traveler
rehearses a single sequence.
Towards evening
on the threshold of a redwood grove
I am barred by white beams
striding from sky
to my path of soft needles and shed bark,
day ending in fire
that does not consume.
Burning forest trunks ascend
without twists of contest, confident
the light will make room.

To see the crowns of such trees,
bare the throat in supplication.
Ladder doorway.
I climb the scorched path.

APPROACHING BLINDNESS

Given clear horizon, the erratic
lenses of my eyes follow a slow blue
crescent of darkness ascending. Steepness
of the meadow slope dissolves in earth's
shadow — tonight rotates into view.

Edges lose power. Cataracts shatter
the naked geometry of the moon
into brushstrokes of luminous scribble.
Sure of my field as any blade of grass,
I take no care. Breathing is sight re-tuned:

September odors of earth after rain
reveal roots alive with tilling motion.
It is not the bird I see, talons fast
within a weave of scrub twigs, but its dart
into flight — scrim of leaf in commotion,

skin's prickle — as though a night spider's first
thread has been cast as far as it may go.
I lift my face to tracking calls of crows,
to keys of black wings releasing tumblers
beyond our web of sky. Not a wing stumbles.

JUDY SEIGEL is a New York City-based artist, former painter, now photographer whose current work combines gum bichromate, and "obsolete" photo process done in paint with other media. She is now editing a new quarterly, *The World Journal of Post-Factory Photography.*

CHARLOTTE MANDEL is the author of *The Life of Mary* (with foreword by Sandra M. Gilbert) and *The Marriages of Jacob* (poem-novellas re-visioning biblical women); *Keeping Him Alive*, *Doll*, and *A Disc of Clear Water*. She coordinated the Eileen W. Barnes Award Series of first books by women poets over 40, and edited the 1982 anthology *Saturday's Women* (coedited by Maxine Silverman and Rachel Hadas). As an independent scholar, she has published articles on the role of cinema in the life and work of the poet H. D. (Hilda Doolittle), and studies of May Sarton.

She currently teaches poetry writing at Barnard College Center for Research on Women.

typographic design: Barbara Bergeron

cover design: Faye Maxwell

MIDMARCH ARTS BOOKS

Documenting Women in the Arts

Gumbo Ya Ya: Anthology of Contemporary African-American
Women Artists

Women Artists of Italian Futurism — Almost Lost to History

Expanding Circles: Women, Art & Community

Camera Fiends and Kodak Girls II: 60 Selections By and About
Women in Photography 1855-1965

Camera Fiends and Kodak Girls I: 50 Selections By and About
Women in Photography 1840-1930

The Heart of the Question: Writings & Paintings of Howardena Pindell

Michelangelo and Me: Six Years in My Italian Haven

The Lady Architects: Lois Lilley Howe, Eleanor Manning,
and Mary Almy, 1893-1937

Modernism & Beyond: Women Artists of the Pacific Northwest

Yesterday and Tomorrow: California Women Artists

No Bluebonnets, No Yellow Roses: Texas Women in the Arts

Pilgrims and Pioneers: New England Women in the Arts

Women Artists of the World

American Women Artists: Works on Paper

When Even the Cows Were Up: Drawings & Stories of an
Artist's Life Spanning the 20th century

— History —

Tarnished Silver: After the Photo Boom,
Essays on Photography 1979-1989

Beyond Walls and Wars: Art, Politics, and Multiculturalism

Mutiny and the Mainstream: Talk That Changed Art, 1975-1990

— Poetry and Images—

Sight Lines

Whirling Round the Sun

Parallels: 3 Artists/ 47 Women Poets

Illuminations: Images for "Asphodel, That Greeny Flower"

Images From Dante

Voices of Women: 3 critics on 3 poets on 3 artists/heroines

— Creatures —

Artists and Their Cats

The Little Cat Who Had No Name

— Information —

Artists Colonies, Retreats & Study Centers

Whole Arts Directory

Guide to Women's Art Organizations and Directory for the Arts